Adult MAD LIBS®

The world's greatest _party_ game

somee cards **Mad Libs**

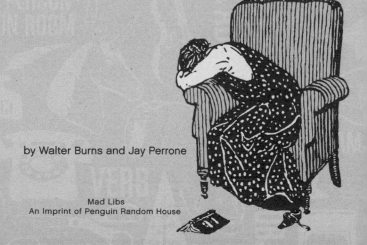

by Walter Burns and Jay Perrone

Mad Libs
An Imprint of Penguin Random House

MAD LIBS
An Imprint of Penguin Random House LLC

Mad Libs format copyright © 2014 by Penguin Random House LLC. All rights reserved.

Concept created by Roger Price & Leonard Stern

The Someecards wordmark and logo are trademarks of Someecards, Inc. and are used under license by
Penguin Random House LLC. Text, images, and artwork are the copyrighted property of Someecards, Inc.
All rights reserved.

Published by Mad Libs,
an imprint of Penguin Random House LLC,
345 Hudson Street, New York, New York 10014.
Printed in the USA.

ISBN 9780843180749

11

Adult MAD LIBS INSTRUCTIONS

The world's greatest _party_ game

MAD LIBS® is a game for people who don't like games!
It can be played by one, two, three, four, or forty.

• RIDICULOUSLY SIMPLE DIRECTIONS

In this book, you'll find stories containing blank spaces where words are left out. One player, the READER, selects one of the stories. The READER shouldn't tell anyone what the story is about. Instead, the READER should ask the other players, the WRITERS, to give words to fill in the blank spaces in the story.

• TO PLAY

The READER asks each WRITER in turn to call out words—adjectives or nouns or whatever the spaces call for—and uses them to fill in the blank spaces in the story. The result is your very own MAD LIBS! Then, when the READER reads the completed MAD LIBS to the other players, they will discover they have written a story that is fantastic, screamingly funny, shocking, silly, crazy, or just plain dumb—depending on the words each WRITER called out.

• EXAMPLE (*Before* and *After*)

" _____ !" he said _____
     EXCLAMATION   ADVERB

as he jumped into his convertible _____ and
      NOUN

drove off with his _____ wife.
      ADJECTIVE

" _____*Ouch*_____ !" he said _____*stupidly*_____
     EXCLAMATION   ADVERB

as he jumped into his convertible _____*cat*_____ and
      NOUN

drove off with his _____*brave*_____ wife.
      ADJECTIVE

In case you have forgotten what adjectives, adverbs, nouns, and verbs are, here is a quick review:

An **ADJECTIVE** describes something or somebody. *Lumpy, soft, ugly, messy,* and *short* are adjectives.

An **ADVERB** tells how something is done. It modifies a verb and usually ends in "ly." *Modestly, stupidly, greedily,* and *carefully* are adverbs.

A **NOUN** is the name of a person, place, or thing. *Sidewalk, umbrella, bridle, bathtub,* and *nose* are nouns.

A **VERB** is an action word. *Run, pitch, jump,* and *swim* are verbs. Put the verbs in past tense if the directions say **PAST TENSE**. *Ran, pitched, jumped,* and *swam* are verbs in the past tense.

When we ask for **A PLACE**, we mean any sort of place: a country or city (*Spain, Cleveland*) or a room (*bathroom, kitchen*).

An **EXCLAMATION** or **SILLY WORD** is any sort of funny sound, gasp, grunt, or outcry, like *Wow!, Ouch!, Whomp!, Ick!,* and *Gadzooks!*

When we ask for specific words, like a **NUMBER**, a **COLOR**, an **ANIMAL**, or a **PART OF THE BODY**, we mean a word that is one of those things, like *seven, blue, horse,* or *head*.

When we ask for a **PLURAL**, it means more than one. For example, *cat* pluralized is *cats*.

MAD LIBS® is fun to play with friends, but you can also play it by yourself! To begin with, DO NOT look at the story on the page below. Fill in the blanks on this page with the words called for. Then, using the words you have selected, fill in the blank spaces in the story. Now you've created your own hilarious MAD LIBS® game!

PERSON IN ROOM __ALISON__

PLURAL NOUN __BALLOONS__

ADJECTIVE __SEXY__

NUMBER __THIRTY-SEVEN__

VERB __DANCE__

NOUN __TROPHY__

LAST NAME __MACINTOSH__

NOUN __HAND-SANITIZER__

ADVERB __MERRILY__

VERB ENDING IN "ING" __CANOODLING__

ADVERB __GRACEFULLY__

ADJECTIVE __UGLY__

VERB __FROLICK__

PART OF THE BODY __PELVIS__

I love you, _____, because you get me. We don't

    PERSON IN ROOM

need to exchange _____ every year or call each other on

              PLURAL NOUN

our birthdays. We both know how _____ our friendship

                            ADJECTIVE

is. Maybe it's because we've known each other for _____

                                           NUMBER

years (or because you saw me _____ that _____

                       VERB   NOUN

and never told anybody), but I trust you more than President

_____ trusts his chief of _____. And it's not just

LAST NAME   NOUN

that you _____ understand where I'm _____ from.

      ADVERB   VERB ENDING IN "ING"

You _____ complement my laziness, and I complement

      ADVERB

yours. You really are the most _____ friend that anyone

                          ADJECTIVE

could ask for. And by "friend," I mean "person who I occasionally

_____ with on _____-book."

VERB   PART OF THE BODY

Adult MAD LIBS® SICK DAYS

The world's greatest _party_ game

MAD LIBS® is fun to play with friends, but you can also play it by yourself! To begin with, DO NOT look at the story on the page below. Fill in the blanks on this page with the words called for. Then, using the words you have selected, fill in the blank spaces in the story. Now you've created your own hilarious MAD LIBS® game!

NOUN ___CANISTER___

VERB ENDING IN "ING" ___RUNNING___

ADVERB ___SADLY___

PERSON IN ROOM (MALE) ___DR. POULOS___

TYPE OF LIQUID ___BLOOD___

ANIMAL ___SLOTH___

VERB ENDING IN "ING" ___SMILING___

NOUN ___BEDPAN___

ADVERB ___SWIMMINGLY___

ADJECTIVE ___BLAND___

NOUN ___TENNIS RACKET___

VERB ___FEAST___

ADVERB ___GROTESQUELY___

EXCLAMATION ___GADZOOKS!___

NOUN ___WHEEL___

OCCUPATION ___GARBAGE COLLECTOR___

Adult MAD LIBS®

SICK DAYS

The world's greatest _party_ game

Me: Hey, man. I swear. This time I'm actually sick! Put the boss on

the _____ so I can tell him I'm not _____ in today.

NOUN   VERB ENDING IN "ING"

You: Okay, but I'm warning you. He _____ won't believe

ADVERB

you, especially after what you did on Saint _____'s Day.

PERSON IN ROOM (MALE)

Me: I was sick then, too! Sure, it was because I drank ten

_____ bombs, but I was still sick as a/an _____

TYPE OF LIQUID   ANIMAL

nonetheless.

You: You're not _____ your case here.

VERB ENDING IN "ING"

Me: Look, I have a/an _____ from my doctor _____

NOUN   ADVERB

stating that I suffer from _____-_____-_____

ADJECTIVE   NOUN   VERB

syndrome. Does that sound like something I made up?

You: It _____ does.

ADVERB

Me: _____. Fine. I'll go into the office, but if I die sitting at

EXCLAMATION

my _____, he's going to hear from my _____.

NOUN   OCCUPATION

Adult MAD/LIBS

GRADUATION DAY

The world's greatest _party_ game

MAD LIBS® is fun to play with friends, but you can also play it by yourself! To begin with, DO NOT look at the story on the page below. Fill in the blanks on this page with the words called for. Then, using the words you have selected, fill in the blank spaces in the story. Now you've created your own hilarious MAD LIBS® game!

ADJECTIVE _____

NUMBER _____

PART OF THE BODY (PLURAL) _____

ADJECTIVE _____

SILLY WORD _____

NOUN _____

ADJECTIVE _____

ADVERB _____

A PLACE _____

ADJECTIVE _____

PLURAL NOUN _____

NOUN _____

TYPE OF LIQUID _____

VERB (PAST TENSE) _____

PERSON IN ROOM (FEMALE) _____

PART OF THE BODY _____

Adult MAD LIBS

GRADUATION DAY

The world's greatest _party_ game

Graduates, congratulations on all your _____ achievements
                                         ADJECTIVE

from the past _____ years! It seems like only yesterday that you
                  NUMBER

were freshmen, or what upperclassmen might call "_____."
                                                   PART OF THE BODY (PLURAL)

Just kidding! Now, I know our guest speaker isn't some _____
                                                          ADJECTIVE

celebrity like _____ from _Jersey_ _____. A lesser
                 SILLY WORD   NOUN

school might have brought someone of her _____ caliber to
                                            ADJECTIVE

be _____ "cool" and "hip." But we, the University of (the)
      ADVERB

_____, felt that having the president of _____
   A PLACE   ADJECTIVE

_____, a highly respected _____ start-up, would be more
  PLURAL NOUN   NOUN

beneficial to you than someone who drank gallons of _____
                                                       TYPE OF LIQUID

and got _____ by the police on national television. So, without
          VERB (PAST TENSE)

further ado, I'd like to welcome _____. Give her a/an
                                   PERSON IN ROOM (FEMALE)

_____!
  PART OF THE BODY

Adult MAD LIBS — E-LOVE FOR MOTHER'S DAY

The world's greatest _party_ game

MAD LIBS® is fun to play with friends, but you can also play it by yourself! To begin with, DO NOT look at the story on the page below. Fill in the blanks on this page with the words called for. Then, using the words you have selected, fill in the blank spaces in the story. Now you've created your own hilarious MAD LIBS® game!

PERSON IN ROOM (FEMALE) _____

ADJECTIVE _____

VERB _____

ADJECTIVE _____

ADVERB _____

NOUN _____

A PLACE _____

NOUN _____

VERB (PAST TENSE) _____

PART OF THE BODY _____

SILLY WORD _____

ADJECTIVE _____

NOUN _____

ADJECTIVE _____

VERB _____

NOUN _____

ADJECTIVE _____

PERSON IN ROOM (MALE) _____

To: _____-1958@mail.com
PERSON IN ROOM (FEMALE)

From: LittleJoey@mail.com

Mom,

Happy Mother's Day! It sure is _____ that we no longer
ADJECTIVE

have to _____ our feelings for each other in person on this
VERB

_____ day. Technology is _____ awesome! I mean,
ADJECTIVE   ADVERB

I am sending this message to you from my e-_____ in
NOUN

(the) _____, but I could have just as easily sent you a/an
A PLACE

_____ on Twitter or _____ on your _____-
NOUN   VERB (PAST TENSE)   PART OF THE BODY

book wall. I wish I could set up a video chat on _____, but
SILLY WORD

my camera isn't working and I can only hear _____ sounds.
ADJECTIVE

I think I need to get it looked at by the Geek _____ at
NOUN

_____ Buy.
ADJECTIVE

Gotta run. Can't wait to _____ you next month at the
VERB

_____ reunion!
NOUN

Your _____ son,
ADJECTIVE

_____
PERSON IN ROOM (MALE)

MAD LIBS® is fun to play with friends, but you can also play it by yourself! To begin with, DO NOT look at the story on the page below. Fill in the blanks on this page with the words called for. Then, using the words you have selected, fill in the blank spaces in the story. Now you've created your own hilarious MAD LIBS® game!

PERSON IN ROOM (MALE) _____

NOUN _____

ADJECTIVE _____

PLURAL NOUN _____

ADJECTIVE _____

VERB ENDING IN "ING" _____

ADJECTIVE _____

PART OF THE BODY _____

NOUN _____

NOUN _____

ANIMAL _____

ARTICLE OF CLOTHING _____

NOUN _____

ADJECTIVE _____

NOUN _____

VERB _____

EXCLAMATION _____

WORKING OUT AT THE OFFICE

The world's greatest _party_ game

_____, good to see you. Take a/an _____.
PERSON IN ROOM (MALE)   NOUN

_____ chair, isn't it? Listen, the reason I called you into my
ADJECTIVE

office today is that we've been receiving some _____ from
                                                PLURAL NOUN

the staff regarding the _____ workout routines you've been
                          ADJECTIVE

_____ around here. For example, doing some _____
VERB ENDING IN "ING"   ADJECTIVE

stretches every now and again is great for your health. Sitting on your

_____ hunched over a/an _____ all day is not great
PART OF THE BODY   NOUN

for your posture, after all. However, taking out a yoga _____
                                                          NOUN

and doing downward-facing-_____ pose without your
                            ANIMAL

_____ on is going a bit too far. Also, bringing in dumbbells
ARTICLE OF CLOTHING

and doing curls during _____ meetings might be frowned
                         NOUN

upon. Please don't think we don't want you to be _____ and
                                                    ADJECTIVE

fit. Just try to adjust your habits while you're working here, okay? Wait,

what are you doing? Why are you _____-pressing my chair?
                                   NOUN

Please _____ that down. Oh _____. Security!
         VERB   EXCLAMATION

MAD LIBS® is fun to play with friends, but you can also play it by yourself! To begin with, DO NOT look at the story on the page below. Fill in the blanks on this page with the words called for. Then, using the words you have selected, fill in the blank spaces in the story. Now you've created your own hilarious MAD LIBS® game!

VERB ENDING IN "ING" _____

ANIMAL (PLURAL) _____

ADJECTIVE _____

NOUN _____

ADJECTIVE _____

NUMBER _____

PART OF THE BODY (PLURAL) _____

PART OF THE BODY (PLURAL) _____

NOUN _____

NUMBER _____

PLURAL NOUN _____

ADJECTIVE _____

NOUN _____

VERB ENDING IN "ING" _____

ADJECTIVE _____

Adult MAD LIBS

The world's greatest *party* game

TRAVEL ETIQUETTE

You'll notice, gentlemen, that I am _____ whilst you all remain
                                    VERB ENDING IN "ING"

seated. Please, don't get up now. If I have to tell you _____
                                                        ANIMAL (PLURAL)

how to behave, it sort of ruins it, don't you think? But since no one has

taught you any _____ manners, allow me to help. Here's a list
                ADJECTIVE

of people for whom you should always give up your _____ on
                                                  NOUN

public transportation.

- The Pregnant: Poor, _____ things have to waddle around
                      ADJECTIVE

  with _____-pound _____. They deserve to
       NUMBER   PART OF THE BODY (PLURAL)

  rest their _____. Also, it's better to assume that a
             PART OF THE BODY (PLURAL)

  "shapely" lady is with _____ than to ask and be wrong!
                         NOUN

- The Elderly: Think about how you will feel _____ years
                                             NUMBER

  from now. Like a pile of _____, that's how! Paying respect
                           PLURAL NOUN

  to those who came before you shows _____ sense.
                                     ADJECTIVE

- The Handicapped: Whether they're in a/an _____ or
                                           NOUN

  _____ on crutches, be a dear and offer your seat.
  VERB ENDING IN "ING"

- The Really Hot: I mean, they're more attractive than you, no

  offense. Why shouldn't they be _____ when they travel?
                                 ADJECTIVE

MAD LIBS® is fun to play with friends, but you can also play it by yourself! To begin with, DO NOT look at the story on the page below. Fill in the blanks on this page with the words called for. Then, using the words you have selected, fill in the blank spaces in the story. Now you've created your own hilarious MAD LIBS® game!

EXCLAMATION _____

NOUN _____

PERSON IN ROOM (MALE) _____

ADJECTIVE _____

COLOR _____

ADVERB _____

NOUN _____

NOUN _____

VERB ENDING IN "ING" _____

NOUN _____

PART OF THE BODY _____

ADJECTIVE _____

ADJECTIVE _____

VERB ENDING IN "ING" _____

ADVERB _____

NUMBER _____

PERSON IN ROOM (FEMALE) _____

Adult MAD LIBS® — THE RIGHT NAME

The world's greatest _party_ game

_____! That was quite a/an _____-making session.
_____ EXCLAMATION _____ NOUN

You are such a lothario, _____. With your _____
PERSON IN ROOM (MALE) ADJECTIVE

_____ hair and that _____ distinguished _____
COLOR ADVERB NOUN

on your face, you are the _____ of masculinity. I'd imagine
NOUN

you are _____ off ladies with a/an _____ as they vie
VERB ENDING IN "ING" NOUN

for your attention. Now don't you go and get a big _____
PART OF THE BODY

over all this praise I'm giving you, sir! Your humility is one of your

_____ qualities, much like your _____ memory. After
ADJECTIVE ADJECTIVE

so many women, the fact that you remembered my name during our

love-_____ is impressive, and I thank you for it. You are so
VERB ENDING IN "ING"

charming that I am going to _____ ignore the fact that I,
ADVERB

along with the last _____ women you've dated, are all named
NUMBER

_____!
PERSON IN ROOM (FEMALE)

MAD LIBS® is fun to play with friends, but you can also play it by yourself! To begin with, DO NOT look at the story on the page below. Fill in the blanks on this page with the words called for. Then, using the words you have selected, fill in the blank spaces in the story. Now you've created your own hilarious MAD LIBS® game!

PERSON IN ROOM (FEMALE) _____

PERSON IN ROOM (MALE) _____

NUMBER _____

ADJECTIVE _____

VERB _____

NOUN _____

NOUN _____

ADJECTIVE _____

EXCLAMATION _____

VERB (PAST TENSE) _____

ADVERB _____

ADJECTIVE _____

VERB _____

ADJECTIVE _____

PLURAL NOUN _____

NUMBER _____

Adult MAD LIBS

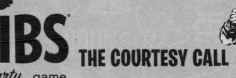

The world's greatest _party_ game

THE COURTESY CALL

Hey, _____? It's me, _____. Yes, I know

PERSON IN ROOM (FEMALE)   PERSON IN ROOM (MALE)

I've been avoiding you for the past _____ days, but there

NUMBER

is a totally _____ explanation for that: I think we should

ADJECTIVE

_____ other people. I also think you should be grateful

VERB

that I am telling you this over the _____ and not with

NOUN

a text message. I am a very busy _____, but I felt you

NOUN

deserved better than a/an _____ message over social media.

ADJECTIVE

_____! Do you remember my last girlfriend? I _____

EXCLAMATION   VERB (PAST TENSE)

her with a tweet! So in your case, I feel I am being _____

ADVERB

generous, _____, and adult about this whole thing . . . even

ADJECTIVE

though we _____ at the same office and will probably have

VERB

a totally _____ encounter tomorrow. Just please make sure

ADJECTIVE

to have those _____ on my desk in time for the meeting at

PLURAL NOUN

_____ o'clock, okay?

NUMBER

MAD LIBS® is fun to play with friends, but you can also play it by yourself! To begin with, DO NOT look at the story on the page below. Fill in the blanks on this page with the words called for. Then, using the words you have selected, fill in the blank spaces in the story. Now you've created your own hilarious MAD LIBS® game!

NOUN _____

PLURAL NOUN _____

ADJECTIVE _____

ADJECTIVE _____

NUMBER _____

PLURAL NOUN _____

ADJECTIVE _____

NOUN _____

VERB ENDING IN "ING" _____

ADJECTIVE _____

ADJECTIVE _____

NOUN _____

PLURAL NOUN _____

ADJECTIVE _____

NOUN _____

Adult MAD LIBS
LOVING YOU OVER LOVING ME

The world's greatest *party* game

My sweet _____, as you know, I used to have a "problem" with
NOUN

watching a lot of adult _____ on the Internet. All of my family
PLURAL NOUN

members, close friends, and doctors agreed that my _____ habit
ADJECTIVE

was not what you'd call "_____ behavior." Plus, I was spending
ADJECTIVE

_____ dollars a week on moisturizer alone! At that rate, I'd never
NUMBER

finish paying off my student _____. Just when I thought
PLURAL NOUN

all was lost, a totally _____ thing happened: You came into
ADJECTIVE

my _____, and it's never been the same. Gone are the days
NOUN

spent _____ in front of my computer. Now, you and I take
VERB ENDING IN "ING"

_____ walks in the park, eat _____ cuisine, and see movies
ADJECTIVE   ADJECTIVE

at the local _____. Plus, I've saved enough _____ to
NOUN   PLURAL NOUN

buy you this _____ diamond ring! So . . . what do you say?
ADJECTIVE

Make me the luckiest _____ alive and marry me?
NOUN

Adult MAD/LIBS

The world's greatest _party_ game

DON'T WORRY, WE'RE ALL SLOWLY DYING

MAD LIBS® is fun to play with friends, but you can also play it by yourself! To begin with, DO NOT look at the story on the page below. Fill in the blanks on this page with the words called for. Then, using the words you have selected, fill in the blank spaces in the story. Now you've created your own hilarious MAD LIBS® game!

PERSON IN ROOM (MALE) _____

PART OF THE BODY _____

ADJECTIVE _____

ADJECTIVE _____

ADVERB_____

NOUN _____

ADJECTIVE _____

ADJECTIVE _____

NOUN _____

VERB_____

NUMBER_____

ADJECTIVE _____

ADJECTIVE _____

TYPE OF LIQUID _____

ADJECTIVE _____

Listen, _____, I'm not going to sit here and lie to

PERSON IN ROOM (MALE)

your _____. Everybody knows that things are really

PART OF THE BODY

_____ nowadays, but I've got some _____ news: We're

ADJECTIVE · ADJECTIVE

all _____ dying, and there is not a/an _____ you

ADVERB · NOUN

can do about it. I know—it's a relief, right? When you think about

it, there's no point in getting all hung up about your _____

ADJECTIVE

job and _____ relationship. Worrying about the state of your

ADJECTIVE

_____ isn't going to help a thing. So why not _____

NOUN · VERB

back and enjoy life while you can? After all, we've got _____-

NUMBER

inch hi-def TVs, _____ phones that can answer every

ADJECTIVE

_____ question in the universe, and six-packs of delicious

ADJECTIVE

_____. How _____ could life be?!

TYPE OF LIQUID · ADJECTIVE

MAD LIBS® is fun to play with friends, but you can also play it by yourself! To begin with, DO NOT look at the story on the page below. Fill in the blanks on this page with the words called for. Then, using the words you have selected, fill in the blank spaces in the story. Now you've created your own hilarious MAD LIBS® game!

ADJECTIVE _____

VERB ENDING IN "ING" _____

NOUN _____

NOUN _____

ADJECTIVE _____

VERB _____

PLURAL NOUN _____

PERSON IN ROOM _____

ADVERB _____

ADJECTIVE _____

ADJECTIVE _____

PLURAL NOUN _____

VERB ENDING IN "ING" _____

NOUN _____

NOUN _____

Adult MAD/LIBS

BUDGET ADVICE

The world's greatest _party_ game

You've just landed a/an _____ job _____ at a public
               ADJECTIVE   VERB ENDING IN "ING"

school. Unfortunately, you're still paying off your _____ loans
                                         NOUN

and living in your grandparents' _____. As someone who's
                                   NOUN

been there, too, here are three tips that'll teach you to live on a/an

_____ salary:
ADJECTIVE

1. Apartments——Live in cheaper areas around the city. Yes, you will

    have to triple-_____ your door, but you'll be saving a ton of
                   VERB

    _____ on rent.
    PLURAL NOUN

2. Furniture—Skip the lines at _____'s Discount Furniture
                                   PERSON IN ROOM

    and go Dumpster shopping. All of your furniture will fall apart

    faster than you can say "I'm broke!" but you'll _____ find
                                            ADVERB

    out how little time you actually spend in your _____
                                                 ADJECTIVE

    apartment anyway.

3. Fun—You probably want to spend your _____ free time
                                         ADJECTIVE

    hanging out with your _____ at bars, but _____
                            PLURAL NOUN   VERB ENDING IN "ING"

    all night can be expensive. Why not do something productive with

    your spare _____, like applying for _____ school?
                     NOUN   NOUN

Adult
MAD/LIBS

A FRATERNITY'S INTERVENTION

The world's greatest _party_ game

MAD LIBS® is fun to play with friends, but you can also play it by yourself! To begin with, DO NOT look at the story on the page below. Fill in the blanks on this page with the words called for. Then, using the words you have selected, fill in the blank spaces in the story. Now you've created your own hilarious MAD LIBS® game!

PERSON IN ROOM (MALE) _____

ADJECTIVE _____

VERB _____

ADJECTIVE _____

NOUN _____

NOUN _____

VERB ENDING IN "ING" _____

PLURAL NOUN _____

A PLACE _____

ADJECTIVE _____

NOUN _____

ADJECTIVE _____

ADJECTIVE _____

NUMBER _____

ADJECTIVE _____

PLURAL NOUN _____

TYPE OF LIQUID _____

ADJECTIVE _____

Adult MAD LIBS

A FRATERNITY'S INTERVENTION

The world's greatest _party_ game

_____, we're here today because we're your friends, and

PERSON IN ROOM (MALE)

we're concerned about you. We're worried that your part-time job and

commitment to studying are having a/an _____ impact on

ADJECTIVE

your college life, and we can't _____ idly by and watch you suffer

VERB

any longer. Something simply must be done about your _____

ADJECTIVE

job as Head _____ Operator at Burger _____. You're a

NOUN　　　　　　　　　　　　　　　　　NOUN

senior, which means you should be _____ it up and skipping all

VERB ENDING IN "ING"

your _____. Instead, all you do is study in (the) _____

PLURAL NOUN　　　　　　　　　　　　　　　　　A PLACE

and work at that _____ fast-food _____. We cannot

ADJECTIVE　　　　　　　　　　NOUN

let you waste what should be the most _____ year ever. You'll

ADJECTIVE

thank me next year when you're stuck working at that _____

ADJECTIVE

job you already landed at a Fortune _____ company and we're

NUMBER

still here living the _____ life. So close those _____

ADJECTIVE　　　　　　　　　　　　PLURAL NOUN

and crack open a/an _____. Now, isn't that _____?

TYPE OF LIQUID　　　　　　　　　　　ADJECTIVE

Adult MAD LIBS®

SEARCHING WITH REGRET

The world's greatest _party_ game

MAD LIBS® is fun to play with friends, but you can also play it by yourself! To begin with, DO NOT look at the story on the page below. Fill in the blanks on this page with the words called for. Then, using the words you have selected, fill in the blank spaces in the story. Now you've created your own hilarious MAD LIBS® game!

VERB ENDING IN "ING" __BUMPING__

ADJECTIVE __LIVELY__

ADVERB __FORCEFULLY__

EXCLAMATION __ZOINKS!__

NOUN __WITCH__

ADJECTIVE __EXPLOSIVE__

ADJECTIVE __PIMPLY__

SILLY WORD __EXPIE-ALADOCIOUS__

NOUN __REINDEER__

NUMBER __126__

VERB ENDING IN "ING" __SCREAMING__

ANIMAL __SLOTH__

ADJECTIVE __MAJESTICALLY__

NOUN __ROAD__

ADJECTIVE __CHARMING__

ADJECTIVE __DRUNK__

Adult MAD LIBS

SEARCHING WITH REGRET

The world's greatest _party_ game

_____ myself on the Internet is quite possibly the most
_{VERB ENDING IN "ING"}

_____ idea I've ever had. I was _____ curious about
_{ADJECTIVE} _{ADVERB}

what I'd see, but _____! I didn't know there were so many
_{EXCLAMATION}

things online about me. Here's a rundown of all the things I found:

- My first _____ written for the student newspaper. Someone
_{NOUN}

reposted it on their _____ blog as a/an _____
_{ADJECTIVE} _{ADJECTIVE}

example of "How Not to Write." Thanks a lot, _____!
_{SILLY WORD}

- A review of a local production of _____ *on the Roof* that I
_{NOUN}

acted in when I was _____ years old. Apparently, the critic
_{NUMBER}

did not appreciate my _____ voice, likening it to "what
_{VERB ENDING IN "ING"}

a/an _____ sounds like when it's got a/an _____
_{ANIMAL} _{ADJECTIVE}

case of _____ poisoning."
_{NOUN}

- A/An _____ photo of me at the beach, courtesy of my ex,
_{ADJECTIVE}

who said she deleted it.

If I ever want to get a/an _____-paying job, I might have to
_{ADJECTIVE}

change my name!

Adult MAD LIBS

The world's greatest _party_ game

SOME HELPFUL PROFESSIONAL ADVICE

MAD LIBS® is fun to play with friends, but you can also play it by yourself! To begin with, DO NOT look at the story on the page below. Fill in the blanks on this page with the words called for. Then, using the words you have selected, fill in the blank spaces in the story. Now you've created your own hilarious MAD LIBS® game!

PERSON IN ROOM (FEMALE) _____

ADJECTIVE _____

NUMBER _____

ADJECTIVE _____

ADJECTIVE _____

TYPE OF LIQUID _____

ADVERB _____

EXCLAMATION _____

PLURAL NOUN _____

PART OF THE BODY _____

NOUN _____

CELEBRITY _____

VERB _____

PLURAL NOUN _____

ADVERB _____

ADJECTIVE _____

SOME HELPFUL PROFESSIONAL ADVICE

The world's greatest _party_ game

To: _____@work.com
PERSON IN ROOM (FEMALE)

As someone who cares about you and your _____ career at this
ADJECTIVE

Fortune _____ company, I must say I am disappointed in your
NUMBER

behavior at last night's holiday party. Having been _____ once
ADJECTIVE

myself, I'd like to give you some _____ advice.
ADJECTIVE

- Enjoying a drink of _____ is _____ fine. Shouting
TYPE OF LIQUID ADVERB

  "_____! _____!" every time you take a sip is not.
  EXCLAMATION PLURAL NOUN

- Complimenting a fellow coworker is encouraged, but I'd
  recommend not applauding the size of our president's _____,
  PART OF THE BODY
  especially since she recently gave birth to a/an _____.
  NOUN

- Singing _____'s "I Want to _____ You (All Night
  CELEBRITY VERB
  Long)" during karaoke is just a bad idea.

- Vomiting all over my new pair of _____ once the party was
  PLURAL NOUN
  over was not appreciated.

I _____ hope you take these words to heart and conduct
ADVERB

yourself in a more _____ manner next time.
ADJECTIVE

Sincerely, Human Resources

Adult MAD/LIBS — THE BACHELORETTE PARTY

The world's greatest *party* game

MAD LIBS® is fun to play with friends, but you can also play it by yourself! To begin with, DO NOT look at the story on the page below. Fill in the blanks on this page with the words called for. Then, using the words you have selected, fill in the blank spaces in the story. Now you've created your own hilarious MAD LIBS® game!

EXCLAMATION _____

ADJECTIVE _____

ADJECTIVE _____

PART OF THE BODY _____

NOUN _____

NOUN _____

ADVERB _____

ADJECTIVE _____

TYPE OF LIQUID _____

ADJECTIVE _____

NOUN _____

NOUN _____

PLURAL NOUN _____

_____! Here comes a bachelorette party. I just wanted a/an

EXCLAMATION

_____, quiet night, and now I have to deal with this? These

ADJECTIVE

parties always have the same _____ types, too. For example,

ADJECTIVE

there's the bachelorette herself. She's wearing a/an _____

PART OF THE BODY

balloon on her head and is falling off the _____ by the bar. I

NOUN

feel bad for her future _____. Next up is the _____

NOUN ADVERB

eager maid of honor. She's trying to make sure this is "the most

_____ night ever!" It seems like she's had a few too many

ADJECTIVE

glasses of vodka and _____. Finally, there's the _____

TYPE OF LIQUID ADJECTIVE

buzzkill, who hates being there since her _____-friend hasn't

NOUN

proposed to her yet. She's going to nurse a beer all night while futzing

with her i-_____. Now, how many _____ do I have to

NOUN PLURAL NOUN

buy for these girls to get them to leave me alone?

MAD LIBS® is fun to play with friends, but you can also play it by yourself! To begin with, DO NOT look at the story on the page below. Fill in the blanks on this page with the words called for. Then, using the words you have selected, fill in the blank spaces in the story. Now you've created your own hilarious MAD LIBS® game!

PERSON IN ROOM (MALE) _____

PERSON IN ROOM (FEMALE) _____

SILLY WORD _____

PART OF THE BODY _____

ADJECTIVE _____

NUMBER _____

ADVERB _____

ADJECTIVE _____

NOUN _____

PLURAL NOUN _____

VEHICLE _____

VERB _____

Adult MAD LIBS — OLD AND IN LOVE

The world's greatest *party* game

Patient(s) Name(s): _____ and _____
PERSON IN ROOM (MALE)　　　　　　　PERSON IN ROOM (FEMALE)

Age(s): 80 and 81

Report: Medics arrived on the scene to find patients immobile while

in the act of _____. The man threw out his _____,
　　　　　　　　SILLY WORD　　　　　　　　　　　　　　　PART OF THE BODY

but it was not until the woman suffered a/an _____ heart
　　　　　　　　　　　　　　　　　　　　　　　ADJECTIVE

attack that 9-1-_____ was called. Female patient was found
　　　　　　　　NUMBER

breathing _____, but had a/an _____ smile on
　　　　　ADVERB　　　　　　　　　　　ADJECTIVE

her face. Male patient was found clutching a bottle of _____.
　　　　　　　　　　　　　　　　　　　　　　　　　　　NOUN

Patients were seen high-fiving while lying side by side on the

_____ inside the _____ as it drove away.
PLURAL NOUN　　　　　　　VEHICLE

Assessment: Patients are medically cleared to leave. I hope I am able

to _____ that much when I'm their age.
　　　VERB

Adult MAD LIBS

I'M KIND OF TERRIBLE

The world's greatest _party_ game

MAD LIBS® is fun to play with friends, but you can also play it by yourself! To begin with, DO NOT look at the story on the page below. Fill in the blanks on this page with the words called for. Then, using the words you have selected, fill in the blank spaces in the story. Now you've created your own hilarious MAD LIBS® game!

ADJECTIVE _____

ADVERB _____

PLURAL NOUN _____

ADJECTIVE _____

ADJECTIVE _____

NOUN _____

ADJECTIVE _____

NUMBER _____

TYPE OF LIQUID _____

NOUN _____

ADJECTIVE _____

ADVERB _____

ANIMAL _____

PLURAL NOUN _____

ADJECTIVE _____

NOUN _____

Adult
MAD/LIBS®   I'M KIND OF TERRIBLE

The world's greatest _party_ game

Thanks for this _____ meal, Mom. I _____
                      ADJECTIVE   ADVERB

appreciate all you do for me, even though I am a useless sack of

_____. I am still amazed at how _____ your love
   PLURAL NOUN   ADJECTIVE

is for me even after all the _____ stunts I've pulled. For
                                   ADJECTIVE

example, that time I got kicked out of _____ Scouts for that
                                              NOUN

teeny, _____ forest fire. You'd think after _____ years
         ADJECTIVE   NUMBER

in the program I'd know that _____ is flammable! Or that
                                TYPE OF LIQUID

time I accidentally pulled the _____ alarm at school. Oops!
                                      NOUN

But here you are, Mom, making me a/an _____ dinner,
                                            ADJECTIVE

which I will _____ feed to our _____ under the
                  ADVERB   ANIMAL

table. When I grow up and have _____ of my own, I hope
                                    PLURAL NOUN

to have the patience that you do . . . or a/an _____ supply of
                                                    ADJECTIVE

over-the-_____ aspirin.
            NOUN

Adult MAD LIBS

SOMEONE TO MAKE OUT WITH

The world's greatest _party_ game

MAD LIBS® is fun to play with friends, but you can also play it by yourself! To begin with, DO NOT look at the story on the page below. Fill in the blanks on this page with the words called for. Then, using the words you have selected, fill in the blank spaces in the story. Now you've created your own hilarious MAD LIBS® game!

PERSON IN ROOM (MALE) _____

ADJECTIVE _____

ADVERB _____

ADJECTIVE _____

NOUN _____

ADJECTIVE _____

ADJECTIVE _____

PLURAL NOUN _____

NUMBER _____

TYPE OF LIQUID _____

CELEBRITY _____

ADJECTIVE _____

PLURAL NOUN _____

PLURAL NOUN _____

Adult MAD LIBS®

SOMEONE TO MAKE OUT WITH

The world's greatest _party_ game

Hi. I normally don't post on _____ slist, so this is kind of
                             PERSON IN ROOM (MALE)

_____, but it's Friday, so who cares, right?! I'll be _____
ADJECTIVE   ADVERB

honest: I want to get _____ at a bar this weekend and make
                           ADJECTIVE

out with a total stranger. If you're interested, here's how it's going to go

down:

1. We lock eyes from across the crowded _____.
                                              NOUN

2. You walk over to me and use a/an _____ pickup line. We
                                          ADJECTIVE

   sit on the _____ couch in the corner to chat about things
                   ADJECTIVE

   like _____ and baseball.
         PLURAL NOUN

3. I will request exactly _____ shots of _____.
                              NUMBER   TYPE OF LIQUID

   Once they're finished, your cue will be to say, "Did you know that

   _____ had her baby last week?" Then, it's on!
       CELEBRITY

4. At the end of our _____ kiss, we do not exchange
                          ADJECTIVE

   _____; we go our separate ways.
     PLURAL NOUN

If you're out there, I can't wait to hear from you. _____ and
                                                       PLURAL NOUN

kisses!

Adult MAD LIBS — PARTY OF ONE

The world's greatest _party_ game

MAD LIBS® is fun to play with friends, but you can also play it by yourself! To begin with, DO NOT look at the story on the page below. Fill in the blanks on this page with the words called for. Then, using the words you have selected, fill in the blank spaces in the story. Now you've created your own hilarious MAD LIBS® game!

ADVERB _____

ADJECTIVE _____

VERB _____

PLURAL NOUN _____

ADVERB _____

PART OF THE BODY (PLURAL) _____

ADJECTIVE _____

ANIMAL (PLURAL) _____

A PLACE _____

VERB ENDING IN "ING" _____

ADJECTIVE _____

ADJECTIVE _____

ADJECTIVE _____

ADJECTIVE _____

PERSON IN ROOM _____

SAME PERSON IN ROOM _____

ADJECTIVE _____

TYPE OF LIQUID _____

You are _____ invited to a/an _____ celebration
          ADVERB   ADJECTIVE

of two people making a commitment to move on with their lives

without each other. Please join us this Saturday as we _____
                                                              VERB

and dance with our closest friends and _____ to ring in our
                                         PLURAL NOUN

divorce. We have had a/an _____ good run, but frankly, we're
                              ADVERB

sick of each other's _____. And let's be _____:
                     PART OF THE BODY (PLURAL)   ADJECTIVE

We could both probably do better. There are plenty of _____
                                                        ANIMAL (PLURAL)

in (the) _____, and we have been _____ the same
          A PLACE   VERB ENDING IN "ING"

_____ trout for far too long now. Plus, we'd rather end it
  ADJECTIVE

on a/an _____ note than wait until we're both too old and
         ADJECTIVE

_____ to meet somebody else! We don't have kids to worry
  ADJECTIVE

about, either, just our _____ goldfish, _____, and
                          ADJECTIVE   PERSON IN ROOM

he will split his time between us. It's a win-win situation for everybody,

especially _____! So please, don't be _____ about
            SAME PERSON IN ROOM   ADJECTIVE

the end of our marriage. Be sad if we run out of _____!
                                                  TYPE OF LIQUID

Adult
MAD LIBS
FANTASY AND FOOTBALL

The world's greatest _party_ game

MAD LIBS® is fun to play with friends, but you can also play it by yourself! To begin with, DO NOT look at the story on the page below. Fill in the blanks on this page with the words called for. Then, using the words you have selected, fill in the blank spaces in the story. Now you've created your own hilarious MAD LIBS® game!

PERSON IN ROOM (MALE) _____

NOUN _____

EXCLAMATION _____

VERB ENDING IN "ING" _____

ADVERB _____

SILLY WORD _____

ADJECTIVE _____

ADJECTIVE _____

VERB _____

ADJECTIVE _____

Adult MAD LIBS® FANTASY AND FOOTBALL

The world's greatest _party_ game

_____, why don't you turn your computer off and stop
PERSON IN ROOM (MALE)

setting your lineup for this week, and we'll go have a fantasy of our own

in the _____-room? No? Okay, then. _____! It seems
NOUN   EXCLAMATION

I'm not _____ any clothes. It's _____ cold in here.
VERB ENDING IN "ING"   ADVERB

Come here and warm me up a bit, huh? Nope. Still ignoring me. What

the _____ is wrong with you? You have a/an _____
SILLY WORD   ADJECTIVE

woman right in front of you, and all you want to do is play with your

_____Internet team?! Fine. If we're not going to _____
ADJECTIVE   VERB

around, at the very least you should swap out your _____end. He
                                                    ADJECTIVE

has a bye this week.

MAD LIBS® is fun to play with friends, but you can also play it by yourself! To begin with, DO NOT look at the story on the page below. Fill in the blanks on this page with the words called for. Then, using the words you have selected, fill in the blank spaces in the story. Now you've created your own hilarious MAD LIBS® game!

NOUN _____

ADJECTIVE _____

PLURAL NOUN _____

NOUN _____

PLURAL NOUN _____

ADJECTIVE _____

PLURAL NOUN _____

ADVERB _____

NOUN _____

VERB _____

NUMBER _____

ANIMAL (PLURAL) _____

ADVERB _____

I ho-ho-hope you like this electronic Christmas _____,
_____NOUN_

because I'm saving our _____ planet. Look at me _not_ using
_____ADJECTIVE_

_____ while the rest of you pollute Mother _____
_PLURAL NOUN_____NOUN_

by spending money on useless _____. Okay, I'm also pretty
_____PLURAL NOUN_

broke. Cards have gotten really _____, huh? Don't get me
_____ADJECTIVE_

wrong, nobody loves Christmas more than I do, but cutting down

acres of defenseless pine _____ to put in our houses? It's
_____PLURAL NOUN_

_____ bad for the planet. That's why I figured it would
ADVERB

be better to send you this e-card of Santa Claus stuck in a/an

_____. Isn't he cute? How did he _____ up there?
_NOUN_____VERB_

Also, can I borrow _____ bucks? C'mon, 'tis the season! I
_____NUMBER_

really need the money to help take care of my _____. They
_____ANIMAL (PLURAL)_

deserve a Christmas, too! And while I'm at it, I should also mention

my rent check is going to be _____ late!
_____ADVERB_